CATHOLIC
PRAYERS AND PRACTICES
for YOUNG DISCIPLES
including
THE ORDER OF MASS

PETER M. ESPOSITO
President

ANNE P. BATTES
Publisher

JO ROTUNNO
Publisher Emeritus

CREDITS AND ACKNOWLEDGMENTS

Copyright © 2015 by RCL Publishing LLC

Send all inquiries to:
RCL Benziger
8805 Governor's Hill Drive, Suite 400
Cincinnati, Ohio 45249

Toll Free 877-275-4725
Fax 800-688-8356
Visit us at **RCLBenziger.com**

978-0-7829-1732-1 (Catholic Prayers and Practices for Young Disciples)
1st Printing
September 2014

General Editor: Mary Malloy
Cover and Page Design: Mary Wessel

ACKNOWLEDGMENTS

Excerpts are taken or adapted from the English translation of the *Roman Missal* © 2010 ICEL; the English translation of the Act of Contrition from *Rite of Penance* © 1974, ICEL; the English translation of *A Book of Prayers* © 1982, ICEL; *Catholic Household Blessings and Prayers* (revised edition) © 2007, United States Conference of Catholic Bishops, Washington, D.C. All rights reserved.

ILLUSTRATION CREDITS

Artwork by Michael O'Neill McGrath, OSFS. Copyright ©2001, 2002, World Library Publications, wlpmusic.com. All rights reserved. Used by permission. Illustrations: Cover, p6, 10, 12, 13, 14, 15, 17, 18, 19, 20, 22, 23, 24, 25, 26, 28, 29, 30, 31, 33, 34, 36, 39, 46, and 48.

© 1994, Archdiocese of Chicago; Liturgy Training Publications, art by Martin Erspamer, OSB. Illustrations: p7, 11, 36, 40, 41, 45, and 47.

p4 © Q2AMedia, p16 ©RCL Benziger.

Dear Child of God,

This small book of prayers will help you when you talk with God. These prayers are prayers that all Catholics pray.

You may use this book to pray with your family, pray quietly by yourself, or with your classmates. You can pray anytime and anywhere.

You may take your small book of prayers with you to Mass. This book will help you follow the Mass. It will also help you pray the prayers we pray together at Mass.

You are a child of God. You are a disciple of Jesus. You are loved.

Your friends and disciples of Jesus,

RCL Benziger
RCLBenziger.com

CATHOLIC
PRAYERS AND PRACTICES

The Sign of the Cross

In the name of the Father,
and of the Son,
and of the Holy Spirit. Amen.

**In the name of
the Father,**

and of the Son,

**and of the
Holy Spirit.**

Amen.

Glory Be (Doxology)

Glory be to the Father
and to the Son
and to the Holy Spirit,
as it was in the beginning
is now, and ever shall be
world without end. Amen.

Our Father (Lord's Prayer)

Our Father, who art in heaven,
hallowed be thy name;
thy kingdom come,
thy will be done
on earth as it is in heaven.
Give us this day our daily bread,
and forgive us our trespasses,
as we forgive those who trespass against us;
and lead us not into temptation,
but deliver us from evil. Amen.

Prayer to the Holy Spirit

Come, Holy Spirit,
   fill the hearts of your faithful.
And kindle in them the fire of your love.
Send forth your Spirit
   and they shall be created.
And you will renew the face of the earth.

Angel of God

Angel of God,
my guardian dear,
to whom God's love commits me here,
ever this day be at my side,
to light and guard, to rule and guide.
Amen.

The Hail Mary

Hail, Mary, full of grace,
the Lord is with thee.
Blessed art thou among women
and blessed is the fruit of thy womb, Jesus.
Holy Mary, Mother of God,
pray for us sinners,
now and at the hour
   of our death.
Amen.

Act of Faith

O my God, I firmly believe that you are one God in three divine Persons, Father, Son, and Holy Spirit; I believe that your divine Son became man and died for our sins, and that he will come to judge the living and the dead. Amen.

Act of Hope

O my God, relying on your infinite goodness and promises, I hope to obtain pardon of my sins, the help of your grace, and life everlasting, through the merits of Jesus Christ, my Lord and Redeemer.
Amen.

Act of Love

O my God, I love you above all things, with my whole heart and soul, because you are all good and worthy of all my love. I love my neighbor as myself for the love of you. I forgive all who have injured me and I ask pardon of all whom I have injured.
Amen.

Morning Prayer

Dear God,
as I begin this day,
keep me in your love and care.
Help me to live as your child today.
Bless me, my family,
   and my friends in all we do.
Keep us all close to you. Amen.

Evening Prayer

Dear God,
I thank you for today.
Keep me safe throughout the night.
Thank you for all the good I did today.
I am sorry for what I have
   chosen to do wrong.
Bless my family and friends.
   Amen.

A Prayer to Follow Jesus

God, I know you will call me
for special work in my life.
Help me follow Jesus each day
and be ready to answer
   your call.
Amen.

Litany of the Saints

Leader: Lord, have mercy
All: **Lord, have mercy**
Leader: Christ, have mercy
All: **Christ have mercy**
Leader: Lord, have mercy
All: **Lord, have mercy**

Holy Mary, Mother of God	pray for us
St. Michael	pray for us
Holy angels of God	pray for us
St. John the Baptist	pray for us
St. Joseph	pray for us
St. Peter and St. Paul	pray for us
St. Andrew	pray for us
St. John	pray for us
St. Mary Magdalene	pray for us
St. Stephen	pray for us
St. Ignatius of Antioch	pray for us
St. Lawrence	pray for us
St. Perpetua and St. Felicity	pray for us
St. Agnes	pray for us
St. Gregory	pray for us
St. Augustine	pray for us
St. Basil	pray for us
St. Martin	pray for us
St. Benedict	pray for us
St. Francis and St. Dominic	pray for us
St. Francis Xavier	pray for us
St. John Vianney	pray for us
St. Catherine	pray for us
St. Teresa of Jesus	pray for us
All you holy men and women	pray for us.

Grace Before Meals

Bless us, O Lord,
and these thy gifts,
which we are about to receive
from thy bounty, through Christ our Lord.
Amen.

Grace After Meals

We give thee thanks, for all thy benefits,
almighty God,
who lives and reigns forever.
Amen.

Prayer of Saint Francis

Lord, make me an instrument
    of your peace:
where there is hatred,
    let me sow love;
where there is injury, pardon;
where there is doubt, faith;
where there is despair, hope;
where there is darkness, light;
where there is sadness, joy.

O divine Master,
    grant that I may not
    so much seek
    to be consoled as to
    console,
to be understood
    as to understand,
to be loved as to love.

For it is in giving that we
    receive,
it is in pardoning that we
    are pardoned,
it is in dying that we are born
    to eternal life.
Amen.

The Angelus

Leader: The Angel of the Lord declared unto Mary,

Response: And she conceived of the Holy Spirit.

All: Hail Mary . . .

Leader: Behold the handmaid of the Lord,

Response: Be it done unto me according to your Word.

All: Hail Mary . . .

Leader: And the Word was made flesh,

Response: And dwelt among us.

All: Hail Mary . . .

Leader: Pray for us, O Holy Mother of God,

Response: That we may be made worthy of the promises of Christ.

All: Amen.

The Golden Rule

Do to others whatever you would have them do to you. This is the law and the prophets.

Matthew 7:12

The Great Commandment

"You shall love the Lord, your God, with all your heart, with all your soul, and with all your mind. . . . You shall love your neighbor as yourself."

Matthew 22:37, 39

The New Commandment

[Jesus said:] "I give you a new commandment: love one another. As I have loved you, so you also should love one another. This is how all will know that you are my disciples, if you have love for one another."

John 13:34-35

The Ten Commandments

1. I am the LORD your God: you shall not have strange gods before me.

2. You shall not take the name of the LORD your God in vain.

3. Remember to keep holy the LORD's Day.

4. Honor your father and your mother.

5. You shall not kill.

6. You shall not commit adultery.

7. You shall not steal.

8. You shall not bear false witness against your neighbor.

9. You shall not covet your neighbor's wife.

10. You shall not covet your neighbor's goods.

The Beatitudes

"Blessed are the poor in spirit,
  for theirs is the kingdom of heaven.
Blessed are they who mourn,
  for they will be comforted.
Blessed are the meek,
  for they will inherit the land.
Blessed are they who hunger
    and thirst for righteousness,
  for they will be satisfied.
Blessed are the merciful,
  for they will be shown mercy.
Blessed are the clean of heart,
  for they will see God.
Blessed are the peacemakers,
  for they will be called children of God.
Blessed are they who are persecuted for the
    sake of righteousness,
  for theirs is the kingdom of
    heaven.
Blessed are you when they insult you
and persecute you and utter every kind
of evil against you [falsely]
because of me. Rejoice and
be glad, for your reward
will be great in heaven."
                    Matthew 5:3-12

15

We pray the
ROSARY

3 Think of the first mystery. Pray an Our Father, 10 Hail Marys, and the Glory Be.

5 Pray the Hail, Holy Queen. Make the Sign of the Cross.

4 Repeat step 3 for each of the next 4 mysteries.

2 Pray an Our Father, 3 Hail Marys, and the Glory Be.

1 Make the Sign of the Cross and pray the Apostles' Creed.

Rosary

Catholics pray the Rosary to honor Mary and remember the important events in the lives of Jesus and Mary. There are twenty mysteries of the Rosary. Follow the steps from 1 to 5.

Joyful Mysteries

1. The Annunciation
2. The Visitation
3. The Nativity
4. The Presentation in the Temple
5. The Finding of the Child Jesus After Three Days in the Temple

Luminous Mysteries

1. The Baptism at the Jordan
2. The Miracle at Cana
3. The Proclamation of the Kingdom and the Call to Conversion
4. The Transfiguration
5. The Institution of the Eucharist

Sorrowful Mysteries

1. The Agony in the Garden
2. The Scourging at the Pillar
3. The Crowning with Thorns
4. The Carrying of the Cross
5. The Crucifixion and Death

Glorious Mysteries

1. The Resurrection
2. The Ascension
3. The Descent of the Holy Spirit at Pentecost
4. The Assumption of Mary
5. The Crowning of the Blessed Virgin as Queen of Heaven and Earth

Hail, Holy Queen

Hail, holy Queen, Mother of mercy:
Hail, our life, our sweetness and our hope.
To you do we cry, poor banished
    children of Eve.
To you do we send up our sighs, mourning
and weeping in this valley of tears.
Turn then, most gracious advocate,
your eyes of mercy toward us;
and after this our exile
show unto us the blessed fruit
    of your womb, Jesus.
O clement, O loving, O sweet Virgin Mary.

Our Lady of Guadalupe

*The Church honors Mary as
Our Lady of Guadalupe. Our
Lady is known by many titles.
Let us honor her as we pray:*

Our Lady of Guadalupe,
pray for us!
Patroness of the Americas,
pray for us!
Patroness of Mexico,
pray for us!
Mother of God,
pray for us!
Queen of peace,
pray for us!

Stations of the Cross

1. Jesus is condemned to death.
2. Jesus accepts his cross.
3. Jesus falls the first time.
4. Jesus meets his mother.
5. Simon helps Jesus carry the cross.
6. Veronica wipes the face of Jesus.
7. Jesus falls the second time.
8. Jesus meets the women.
9. Jesus falls the third time.
10. Jesus is stripped of his clothes.
11. Jesus is nailed to the cross.
12. Jesus dies on the cross.
13. Jesus is taken down from the cross.
14. Jesus is buried in the tomb.

Some parishes end the Stations by reflecting on the Resurrection of Jesus.

✦ BLESSING
PRAYERS

Prayer for Mothers

Dear Jesus,
you loved your mother, Mary,
very much.

Bless my mother.
Help her with the work
she has to do today.

Help me to show her
love and respect
in all I say and do.
Amen.

Prayer for Fathers

Dear Jesus,
you loved and obeyed Joseph,
your father on Earth.

Bless my father.
Help him with the work
he has to do today.

Help me to show him
love and respect
in all I say and do.
Amen.

Blessing of Grandparents

Lord God almighty,
bless our grandparents with long life,
    happiness, and health.
May they remain constant in your love
and be living signs of your presence
to their children and grandchildren.
We ask this through Christ our Lord.
Amen.

Blessing on Birthdays

Loving God,
you created all the people of the world,
and you know each of us by name.
We thank you for _____,
    (pray the person's name)
who celebrates his/her birthday.

Bless him/her with your love and friendship
that he/she may grow in wisdom,
    knowledge, and grace.
May he/she love his/her family always
and be ever faithful to his/her friends.
Grant this through Christ our Lord.
Amen.

Blessing Before First Communion

(Pray the person's name)
_____, may the Lord Jesus touch your
  ears to receive his Word,
and your mouth to proclaim his faith.
May you come with joy to his supper
to the praise and glory of God.
Amen.

Prayer to Begin a School Year

God of wisdom and might,
we praise you for the wonders of our being,
for mind, body, and spirit.
Be with our children as they begin
  a new school year.
Bless them and their teachers and staff.
We ask this through Jesus Christ our Lord.
Amen.

Blessing for a Pet

O God,
you ask us to care for and
to enjoy the creatures
of the earth.
Bless our pet, _____ (name).
Keep him/her safe and healthy.
Help us to care for him/her.
Amen.

THE SEVEN SACRAMENTS

Jesus gave the Church the Seven Sacraments.
They are signs of God's love for us.
When we celebrate the Sacraments,
Jesus is really present with us.
We share in the life of the Holy Trinity.

SACRAMENTS OF INITIATION

Baptism

We are joined to Christ. We become members of the Body of Christ, the Church.

Confirmation

The Holy Spirit strengthens us to live as children of God.

Eucharist

Sharing in the Eucharist joins us most fully to Christ and to the Church. We receive the Body and Blood of Christ.

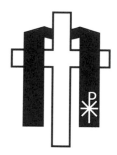

Penance and Reconciliation

Through the ministry of the priest we receive God's gift of forgiveness and peace.

Anointing of the Sick

We receive God's healing strength when we are sick or dying, or weak because of old age.

Holy Orders

A baptized man is ordained to serve the Church as a bishop, priest, or deacon.

Matrimony

A baptized man and a baptized woman make a lifelong promise to love and respect each other as husband and wife. They promise to accept the gift of children from God.

The SACRAMENT of PENANCE and RECONCILIATION

Individual Rite

- Greeting
- Scripture Reading
- Confession of Sins and
    Acceptance of Penance
- Act of Contrition
- Absolution
- Closing Prayer

Communal Rite

- Greeting
- Scripture Reading
- Homily
- Examination of
    Conscience
- Litany of Contrition
    and the Lord's Prayer
- Individual Confession
    and Absolution
- Closing Prayer

Examination of Conscience

Examine your conscience to help you live as a child of God. Ask yourself if you are living as Jesus wants you to live.

Read and think about the questions to help you examine your conscience.

- ❑ Do I talk to God every day?
- ❑ Do I thank God for my gifts and talents?
- ❑ Do I care for the things of the earth?
- ❑ Do I obey my parents and show them respect?
- ❑ Do I listen and show respect to my teachers and principal at school?
- ❑ Do I show respect to my classmates?
- ❑ Do I share what I have with those in need?
- ❑ Do I say I'm sorry to the person I have hurt?
- ❑ Do I say I forgive you to the person who has hurt me?

Think about one way you will live as a child of God tomorrow. Ask the Holy Spirit to help you.

Act of Contrition

My God,
I am sorry for my sins with all my heart.
In choosing to do wrong
and failing to do good,
I have sinned against you
whom I should love above all things.
I firmly intend, with your help,
to do penance,
to sin no more,
and to avoid whatever leads me to sin.
Our Savior Jesus Christ
suffered and died for us.
In his name, my God, have mercy.

The Good Shepherd

Jesus, the Good Shepherd, leads and cares for his sheep. He guides us in ways that are right and good.

A Visit to Church

Catholic churches are built in many styles and sizes. Some Catholic churches are older and some are newer. Some are big and some are small. But, all churches are places where people worship God.

Baptismal Font

As you enter a Catholic church, you may see a baptismal font. The baptismal font holds the water used for the Sacrament of Baptism.

Paschal Candle

The Paschal candle, also called the Easter candle, is a symbol of the Risen Christ who is the Light of the world.

Ambo

The ambo is the special place from where the Word of God is read. The lectors are the people who read the First and Second Readings during Mass. The deacon or priest reads the Gospel.

Altar

The altar is the table from which Jesus shares his Body and Blood with us. It reminds us of the Last Supper and that Jesus died for us.

Crucifix

A crucifix is a cross with an image of Jesus on it. You may see a crucifix carried in procession by one of the altar servers. The crucifix is a sign of God's love and mercy.

Through the Church, Christ continues to be with us in the world. The Church is every one of us, the People of God.

From its beginning the Church has used symbols to help us understand what we believe as Catholics.

Cross

The Cross is one of the most widely used symbols of our faith. It reminds us that Jesus died on the Cross and was raised from the dead.

Dove

The dove is a symbol that is used for the Holy Spirit. It reminds us of the gift of the Holy Spirit, who strengthens us to live our Baptism. The dove is also a symbol for peace.

Water

Water is a symbol of both life and of death. We pray the Sign of the Cross with holy water to remind us of our Baptism.

Holy Oils

There are three holy oils used by the Church. These oils are kept in a special place in the church called an ambry.

The LITURGICAL YEAR

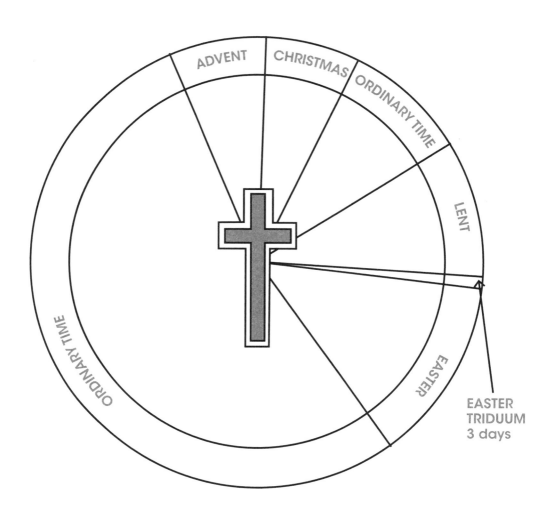

Read page 33. Then color the seasons
of the Church year using the colors,
purple, white, and green.

The Church year of prayer and worship is called the liturgical year.

Advent

Advent begins the Church year. We get our hearts ready to remember the birth of Jesus. The color for Advent is purple.

Christmas

At Christmas, the Church celebrates the birth of Jesus, God's Son. The color for Christmas is white.

Lent

Lent is the time of the Church year when we remember Jesus died for us. It is a time to get ready for Easter. The color for Lent is purple.

Easter

During the Easter season, we celebrate that Jesus was raised from the dead. Jesus gave us the gift of new life. The color for Easter is white.

Ordinary Time

Ordinary Time is the longest time of the Church's year. The color for Ordinary Time is green.

✠ WE CELEBRATE THE MASS

The INTRODUCTORY RITES

We remember that we are the community of the Church. We prepare to listen to the Word of God and to celebrate the Eucharist.

The Entrance

We stand as the priest, deacon, and other ministers enter the assembly. We sing a gathering song. The priest and deacon kiss the altar. The priest then goes to the chair, where he presides over the celebration.

Sign of the Cross and Greeting

The priest leads us in praying the Sign of the Cross. The priest greets us, and we say, **"And with your spirit."**

The Penitential Act

We admit our wrongdoings. We bless God for his mercy. We pray:

Lord, have mercy.
Christ, have mercy.
Lord, have mercy.

Gloria

Glory to God in the highest,
and on earth peace to people of good will.

We praise you,
we bless you,
we adore you,
we glorify you,
we give you thanks for your great glory,
Lord God, heavenly King,
O God, almighty Father.

Lord Jesus Christ, Only Begotten Son,
Lord God, Lamb of God, Son of the Father,
you take away the sins of the world,
    have mercy on us;
you take away the sins of the world,
    receive our prayer;
you are seated at the right hand of the
    Father, have mercy on us.
For you alone are the Holy One,
you alone are the Lord,
you alone are the Most High, Jesus Christ,
with the Holy Spirit,
in the glory of God the Father.
Amen.

The Collect

The priest leads us in praying the Collect.
We respond, **"Amen."**

The LITURGY of the WORD

. . . .

God speaks to us today.
We listen and respond to God's Word.

The First Reading

We sit and listen as the reader reads from the Old Testament or from the Acts of the Apostles. The reader concludes, "The word of the Lord." We respond, **"Thanks be to God."**

The Responsorial Psalm

The cantor leads us in singing a psalm.

The Second Reading

The reader reads from the New Testament, but not from the four Gospels. The reader concludes, "The word of the Lord." We respond, **"Thanks be to God."**

Acclamation

We stand to honor Christ, present with us in the Gospel. The cantor leads us in singing **"Alleluia, Alleluia, Alleluia"** or another chant during Lent.

The Gospel

The deacon or priest proclaims, "A reading from the holy Gospel according to (name of Gospel writer)." We respond, **"Glory to you, O Lord."**

He proclaims the Gospel. At the end, he says, "The Gospel of the Lord." We respond, **"Praise to you, Lord Jesus Christ."**

The Homily

We sit. The priest or deacon preaches the homily. He helps the whole community understand the Word of God spoken to us in the readings.

The Profession of Faith

We stand and profess our faith. We pray the Creed together.

Nicene Creed

I believe in one God,
the Father almighty,
maker of heaven and earth,
of all things visible and invisible.

I believe in one Lord Jesus Christ,
the Only Begotten Son of God,
born of the Father before all ages.
God from God, Light from Light,
true God from true God,
begotten, not made,
   consubstantial with the Father;
through him all things were made.
For us men and for our salvation
he came down from heaven,

*(At the words that follow, up to and
including* and became man, *all bow.)*

and by the Holy Spirit was incarnate of the
   Virgin Mary, and became man.

For our sake he was crucified
   under Pontius Pilate,
he suffered death and was buried,
and rose again on the third day
in accordance with the Scriptures.
He ascended into heaven
and is seated at the right hand of the Father.

He will come again in glory
to judge the living and the dead
and his kingdom will have no end.

I believe in the Holy Spirit, the Lord,
    the giver of life,
who proceeds from the Father
  and the Son,
who with the Father and the
    Son is adored and glorified,
who has spoken through the prophets.

I believe in one, holy, catholic
    and apostolic Church.
I confess one Baptism for the forgiveness
    of sins
and I look forward to the resurrection
    of the dead
and the life of the world to come.
Amen.

Especially during the liturgical seasons of Lent and Easter, the Apostles' Creed may be used in place of the Nicene Creed.

Apostles' Creed

I believe in God,
the Father almighty,
Creator of heaven and earth,
and in Jesus Christ, his only Son, our Lord,

*(At the words that follow, up to and
including* the Virgin Mary, *all bow.)*

who was conceived by the Holy Spirit,
born of the Virgin Mary,
suffered under Pontius Pilate,
was crucified, died and was buried;
he descended into hell;
on the third day he rose again from the dead;
he ascended into heaven,
and is seated at the right hand
    of God the Father almighty;
from there he will come to judge the living
    and the dead.

I believe in the Holy Spirit,
the holy catholic Church,
the communion of saints,
the forgiveness of sins,
the resurrection of the body,
and life everlasting. Amen.

The Prayer of the Faithful

The priest leads us in praying for our Church and her leaders, for our country and its leaders, for ourselves and others, for the sick and those who have died. We can respond to each prayer in several ways. One way we respond is, **"Lord, hear our prayer."**

The LITURGY of the EUCHARIST

*We join with Jesus and the Holy Spirit
to give thanks and praise to God the Father.*

The Preparation of the Altar and Gifts

We sit as the altar is prepared and the collection is taken up. We share our blessings with the community of the Church and especially with those in need. The cantor may lead us in singing a song. The gifts of bread and wine are brought to the altar.

The priest lifts up the bread and blesses God for all our gifts. He prays, "Blessed are you, Lord God of all creation, . . ." We respond, **"Blessed be God for ever."**

The priest lifts up the cup of wine and prays, "Blessed are you, Lord God of all creation, . . ." We respond, **"Blessed be God for ever."**

The priest invites us, "Pray, brethren (brothers and sisters), that my sacrifice and yours may be acceptable to God, the almighty Father."

We stand and respond,
**"May the Lord accept the sacrifice
    at your hands
for the praise and glory of his name,
for our good
and the good of all his holy Church."**

The Prayer over the Offerings

The priest leads us in praying the Prayer over the Offerings. We respond, **"Amen."**

Opening Dialog and Preface

The priest invites us to join in praying the Church's great prayer of praise and thanksgiving to God the Father.

Priest: "The Lord be with you."
Assembly: **"And with your spirit."**
Priest: "Lift up your hearts."
Assembly: **"We lift them up to the Lord."**

Priest: "Let us give thanks to
the Lord our God."
Assembly: "It is right and just."

After the priest sings or prays aloud the
Preface, we acclaim,
**"Holy, Holy, Holy Lord God of hosts.
Heaven and earth are full of your glory.
Hosanna in the highest.
Blessed is he who comes in
the name of the Lord.
Hosanna in the highest."**

The Eucharistic Prayer

The priest leads the assembly in praying the
Eucharistic Prayer. We call upon the Holy
Spirit to make our gifts of bread and wine
holy and that they become the Body and
Blood of Jesus. We recall what happened at
the Last Supper. The bread and wine become
the Body and Blood of the Lord.

Jesus is truly and really present under the
appearances of bread and wine. The priest
sings or says aloud, "The mystery of faith." We
respond using this or another acclamation
used by the Church,

**"We proclaim your Death, O Lord,
and profess your Resurrection
until you come again."**

The priest then prays for the Church. He
prays for the living and the dead.

Doxology

The priest concludes the praying of the
Eucharistic Prayer. He sings or prays aloud,
"Through him, and with him, and in him,
O God, almighty Father,
in the unity of the Holy Spirit,
all glory and honor is yours,
for ever and ever."
We respond, **"Amen."**

The COMMUNION RITE

The Lord's Prayer

We pray the Lord's Prayer together..

The Sign of Peace

The priest invites us to share a sign of peace,
saying, "The peace of the Lord be with you
always." We respond,
> **"And with your spirit."**

We share a sign of peace.

The Fraction, or the Breaking of the Bread

The priest breaks the host, the consecrated bread. We sing or pray aloud,

**"Lamb of God, you take
away the sins of the world,
have mercy on us.
Lamb of God, you take away
the sins of the world,
have mercy on us.
Lamb of God, you take away
the sins of the world,
grant us peace."**

Communion

The priest raises the host and says aloud, "Behold the Lamb of God, behold him who takes away the sins of the world. Blessed are those called to the supper of the Lamb."

We join with him and say,
"Lord, I am not worthy that you should enter under my roof, but only say the word and my soul shall be healed."

The priest receives Communion. Next, the deacon, the extraordinary ministers of Holy Communion, and the members of the assembly receive Communion.

 If we are to receive the Body of Christ, the priest, deacon, or extraordinary minister of Holy Communion holds up the host. We bow and the priest, deacon, or extraordinary minister of Holy Communion says, "The Body of Christ."

We respond, **"Amen."** We then receive the consecrated host in our hand or on our tongue.

If we are to receive the Blood of Christ, the priest, deacon, or extraordinary minister of Holy Communion holds up the cup containing the consecrated wine. We bow and the priest, deacon, or extraordinary minister of Holy Communion says, "The Blood of Christ." We respond, **"Amen."** We take the cup in our hands and drink from it.

The Prayer after Communion

We stand as the priest invites us to pray, saying, "Let us pray." He prays the Prayer after Communion. We respond, **"Amen."**

The CONCLUDING RITES

*We are sent forth to do good works,
praising and blessing the Lord.*

Greeting

We stand. The priest greets us as we prepare to leave. He says, "The Lord be with you." We respond, **"And with your spirit."**

Blessing

The priest or deacon may invite us, "Bow down for the blessing." The priest blesses us, saying, "May almighty God bless you, the Father, and the Son, and the Holy Spirit." We respond, **"Amen."**

Dismissal of the People

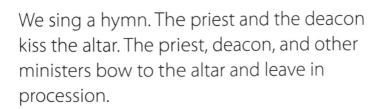

The priest or deacon sends us forth, using these or similar words, "Go and announce the Gospel of the Lord." We respond, **"Thanks be to God."**

We sing a hymn. The priest and the deacon kiss the altar. The priest, deacon, and other ministers bow to the altar and leave in procession.

"Love One Another as I have Loved You."

Go in peace, glorifying the Lord by your life.

Concluding Rites, *Roman Missal*